QUARLL

QUARLL

Chris Considine

PETERLOO POETS

First published in 2006
by Peterloo Poets
The Old Chapel, Sand Lane, Calstock,
Cornwall PL18 9QX, U.K.

© 2006 by Chris Considine

The moral rights of the author are asserted in accordance with the Copyright, Designs and Patent Act, 1988

All rights reserved. No part of this publication may be reproduced, stored in a retrieval system, or transmitted, in any form or by any means, electronic, mechanical, photocopying, recording or otherwise without the prior permission in writing of the publisher.

A catalogue record for this book is available from the British Library

ISBN 1-904324-27-4

Printed in Great Britain by
Antony Rowe Ltd, Chippenham, Wilts.

ACKNOWLEDGEMENTS

"Cuthbert and the Sea Otters" was included in *St Cuthbert and Bystanders* (Redbeck Press, 2001).

The sequence "Heloise Dreaming" was commended in the Writers inc. Competition, 2003.

"Beatrice Harrison Plays her Cello to the Nightingale" was a prizewinner in the Peterloo Poetry Competition, 2004, and "Catching Up" appeared in *The North*, "Dr. Feldheim's Calendar" in *Poetry Nottingham* and "The Fruit-Eaters" in *Other Poetry*.

Many thanks to the founder, trustees and staff of Hawthornden Castle International Retreat for Writers, where I stayed for a month in 2004 and wrote 6 of these poems.

CONTENTS

9	QUARLL
9	1. Hatchet
9	2. Fire
10	3. Hut
11	4. Bow
12	5. Sea
13	6. Antelope
13	7. Monkey
14	8. Planks
15	9. Wives
15	10. Boy
16	11. Vine
17	12. Caves
18	13. Hermit Crab
19	Dr. Feldheim's Calendar
20	Heroes
21	Retreat
22	In Praise of Red Sandstone
23	Beatrice Harrison Plays Her Cello to the Nightingale
24	Face
25	Catching Up
26	Touch
27	Postcards from the Gallery
28	Little Fluffy Goes Native
30	Dissolution
31	Sheep Show
32	The Fruit-Eaters
33	Oh Speak Again, Bright Angel!
34	Lover
35	The Love-Token

36	Washing the Teaset
37	Travelling
38	Christmas Presents
39	Sunday Afternoon
40	Hospital Visit
41	Thistledown
42	Cuthbert and the Sea Otters
43	Setting Out
46	Endings
48	SHAKESPEARE'S LOST LADIES
48	1. Queen Lear
48	2. Donalbain's Mother
49	3. Signora Brabantio
50	4. Lady Polonius
51	5. Duchess of Milan
52	6. Princess Escalus
53	7. Lost Ladies
54	HELOISE DREAMING

QUARLL

Philip Quarll
Born 1647. Shipwrecked 1675. Discovered by Edward Dorrington 1724. Died ?

1. Hatchet

Yes. There. Glossy with wet
the scratched yellow handle
sticking out of the crevice that caught me
shaken from the top of the ship.

In my fist again, and the orange-blotched
steel head still sweetly locked on,
thin line of light still arcing
along the edge in spite of sea-salt.

I remember the wet-wood sting,
the weight in my hand of hatchet
earth-born, fire-shaped, sea-soaked
and flying like a pennant in the gale.

The mast brandished me, clamped
half-conscious against the shrouds,
eyes waterlogged and arm's one aim
to slash sail from the yard.

But the many-headed rock leapt out,
split and splintered the ship. By daylight
shivering on my pinnacle I saw
only anonymous debris face down in the waves.

2. Fire

I struck fire with my knife and flint
and a handful of dead grass. (Later
dried fungus made excellent tinder.)
Set light to the brushwood.
With crackle and gunshot-noise

there was day in darkness,
heat, a kind of conversation,
a loosening of thought.

After-image of blue,
the flame streamed like golden water
from a deck, waved in the air
like shreds of sail,
like drowning hands.

3. Hut

I have lived my life in evil enclosures —
stink of prison, stink of below-decks —

and these two nights in terror, sodden
on a rock, sleepless in a tree.

I want this start to be fresh, clean,
safe from whatever invisibly howls.

From this copse of saplings
I choose four for corners,

gouge pits, plant poles for walls.
This will take days, weeks, years to finish:

the turfed hurdle roof,
the pleaching of my corner trees,

arm reaching out to arm
to fur the sides with living green.

4. Bow

My name is a crossbow bolt, and a crossbow
is what I need, but how can I fashion
the latch and spring of it with knife and hatchet?

The fish-pond thief may be an albatross —
or perhaps not. To me it is only
the enemy, big, quick and deadly.

A branchless bendable stave
is the best I can manage, man-high,
notched at each end; and from the unravelling sail

I twine and rosin the loose thread.
Arrows are whittled sticks, fire-hardened,
fletched with parchment.

Making, practising: puzzle and challenge.
I am absorbed as a child
killing time in his garden.

And proud when the bird bursts from the water
flapping wide wings and scattering brightness,
and I get it first time and through the heart.

All its soaring gone, and it plumps down
on the mud-bank with wings spread out
in the shape of a clumsy cross.

5. Sea

The sea hurts my eyes
with its huge blueness.
Land borders it with black,
horizon with indigo.
Beneath it, pullulating life,
too much, cruel. Concealed
under smoothness.

I lie in wait.
The blue mirror is blank
though I stare at it
until my eyes go dark.
I have built a fire on the cliff
but it is feeble.
Sun and sea have sucked it small.

I nearly miss the ship when it appears.
My eyes refuse to believe —
mirage like a fly brushed off.
And then the heart's jolt,
wood flung on fire,
shirt brandished with cracking arms.
And it vanishes

as if I was invisible,
dead already with my fellows.
I run down knife-blade rocks
screaming into the water
and fight its bulk
to get in further, deeper,
in over my head.

6. Antelope

At last my nets are lucky: two sad antelopes
caught by their corkscrew horns.

I approach them humbly. My hand
rejoices in the shock of warmth,

the beat of blood, the live skin
under the flat fawn hair that lies

tight against muscle. Their dark eyes
are watchful, not fearful. I am Adam, the first man.

They are female, pregnant perhaps. I comb the woods
for vegetable delicacies, lie awake at night

happy to hear their rustle and breathing.
In the morning I inhale their lively scent.

When one gives birth I share her fear,
pain, effort and drowsy pride.

How could I use that miracle as meat?
But milk and cheese I have as my herd increases.

7. Monkey

And then there was the golden monkey,
its leathery concave face. It chose me.
I did not entice it.

Followed me with its shambling gait.
When I gathered wood or fruit
or dug for roots, it copied me.

I called him Beaufidel; he was my shadow
but bright, not dark, his hair standing
like needles of light.

When I sat down he would clasp my shoulder
with his old man's hand. I never caressed him,
had no desire to enthral him.

I killed him though — torn bloodily apart
by his wild cousins. My smell lived on his fur.
I heard his human scream.

8. Planks

My shelves, with their housewifely burdens of pickled
anchovies and mushrooms, sea-salt, antelope milk,

are boards from the dismantled boat, thin oak,
brine-darkened, with a grain like the ripples in sand.

After that storm it was the voice that had me leaping
fearlessly down the rocks, blood turned to liquid fire.

A woman's cry, surely. Eve to my Adam. At once
peace of mind became poverty. Eden was prison.

With the strength of several I heaved up the gunwale,
flung the battered boat on to its flat base.

Disappointment was a blow to the gut, pain
to double me over: a ragged boy babbling in French,

and a jumble of enemy implements — ropes, sodden guns,
crowbar and pickaxe to plunder me with.

Grimly we broke up the holed boat, carried home tools and wood,
while his pirate masters slept under the sea.

9. Wives

His raging wives fall on him
all four at once spitting like cats,
raking him with their nails,
sinking their teeth in.

He bleeds from a hundred punctures.
In parallel tracks and rosettes of teethmarks
his skin burns under a flurry
of shrieks, screams and pummelings.

Judge, jury, a courtroom full of women
all on their feet, all sobbing accusations:
bigamy, cruelty, rape. The boy shakes him
awake to his shaking heart.

When he sleeps again towards dawn
the angelic treble calls him
from under the boat. His first and last
wife, who came back to him in prison.

Her skin is silk under his fingers,
her body smooth and still, cool, and now
vanishing, sewn into a sail
and swallowed by the ocean.

10. Boy

He stank of sweat and terror. I cleaned him up
and shared such clothing as I had —
my washed-thin rags, the robes of plaited grass
woven in winter, one or two pelts.

I fed him, made him a bed by mine.
He was more savage than the woodland beasts.
It took time to tame him, but I was glad
of his human voice, the hard-won smile.

Did my eyeing him make him uncomfortable?
I thought he was held fast here, heir
to my island, stored joy for my final years,
but when I went to look for him, too long bird-nesting,

all I found was the dropped bag, a mess
of broken eggs, and shrinking towards the horizon
a miniature ship, the half-moon stern,
the ranks of tiny sails gilded with sunset.

11. Vine

As seafarer
I knew the meaning of clouds
but not their colours.

Knew tide times and spring tides
but never watched them rising
inch by inch.

I knew the wind's speed
and its direction
but not its different voices.

At first the songs of birds
were a foreign language —
sea-birds, small song-birds,
the great birds that touch hands
in the sky in a swirl of skirts.

The flowers were alien,
waiting for names:
lily-tree, star-bush,
red trumpeter, hairy bell.
Each arrives in its proper order.

All afternoon
I have watched the sunlight
move gradually
through petal and leaf
vivid as windows.

This vine especially
with its green, bronze
and crimson five-fingered
translucent leaves breathing
against the blue.

12. Caves

Caves full of concavities, the grey and purple rock
folded, pitted and fractured. A cough,
here, is a frenzied barking, a sneeze
is a storm-wind in a wood.

I come here to sing with shut eyes and open throat
the psalms and hymns familiar from childhood
but no profane songs, for as soon as I start
an angel echoes me, then another, another,

like bird to bird to bird at sunrise,
a feast of praise. How can the lucky not
believe in providence,
singled out for survival and contentment?

A lonely man will speak aloud to hear
a human voice. I speak or sing
and am in an instant swallowed up
in a thousand-headed chorus.

13. Hermit Crab

Look down, now, into this other world
the low tide left behind.
Through its glassy atmosphere
shrimps glide like denser glass,
fish flash surprisingly
like lights inside the eye.

And look! The hermit crabs
fearful and prudent
scuttle on skinny legs
under their pinnacles and crenellations.
I am a hermit crab, secure now
and fixed in my adopted shell.

*

You offer me a ship, a voyage,
haven for my old age,
but these are siren promises
too late to lure me back.
Dying should be a private matter.
And what death-bed easier than Eden?

Dr. Feldheim's Calendar

Not visited in his cell by angels but by numbers
in their measured dance, cleaner than deeds
or words, bringing the illusion of sanity.

His paces across concrete, multiples of the five
from corner to corner. His pulse-beats
that quickened at the knockings on the wall.

The intensifications of darkness could be called
nights, and counted. And mathematical conundrums
progressed like constellations through his mind.

Afterwards, in a land that was never home,
he was compelled like the ancient mariner
to recount the insults of his fatherland:

annihilated days and months and years,
the never-existing wife and child. To my father,
the spellbound wedding-guest, he gave

a wooden calendar. Four cubes: numbers to ten
(six doubling as nine), Sonntag to Samstag,
Januar to Dezember. All their permutations.

Tokens of lost time and lives. After his death
faithfully every day my father built the date
as a remembrance. Now he too is dead

I rearrange the scratched and battered blocks
to mark their posthumous days when I remember.

Heroes

In the pissing contest, Jack won.
Ann and the girls, secretly shocked,
kept their faces expressionless.
That hot summer Jack went along
Duck Lane with a box of matches.
Jim followed, beating hedge-fires out.
Ann wondered: What if? Didn't God
speak from an orange blazing bush?

Hotter, hotter the desert. Air
like transparent flame and embers
underfoot. No God there with Jim
crisped in the furnace of his tank.
Jack soldiered on to Sicily,
Italy, back home, a hero.

Remembrance Sunday — cold brilliance.
Jack, always chilly, is swaddled,
poppy pinned on his woolly hat
like a head-wound over blank eyes.
He has forgotten how to speak.
And what things does he remember?
Ann pushes the wheelchair grimly
along the uneven tarmac.

Retreat

She called it exile. Is that what it is,
this apartness? We sleep in the attic
but have the run of this grand
castle, its hundred acres. We can walk
through shrubbery, beside the quick river,
along the drive under lordly tall oaks.

The castle is a silent place. Before sunrise
deer stand on the lawn. Our escape
into contemplation is voluntary. Sometimes
it seems we could be the last survivors,
huddled in this place of caves and ruins
largely concealed by vegetation.

Almost an island, but like an island
ringed with all kinds of flotsam:
plastic rubbish in the river; near the gates
ruts and divots in the grass and empty bottles;
beer cans by the ruined cottage — because
the bleak townships are encroaching

just out of sight — and sometimes in the woods
we hear the laughter of feral children.
Newspapers, radio bulletins slip in
like messages in bottles, relatives
still tug at us with letters and phonecalls,
until we feel not so much exiled as besieged.

In Praise of Red Sandstone

I like the uncomplaining nature of rock,
its lack of outcry at finding itself
(once lowest of the low) flung up in air
floodlit by sun. From greyish pallor
turned flesh-pink, orange, golden,
rust, like sunflushed skin.

It doesn't care what words we call it:
bastion, buttress, column; or what profiles
of patriarch or sphinx we think we find in it.
It stands fast, suffers warming and cooling,
greening by moss, blueing by lichen,
shape-shift to tree by ivy.

Grooved , striated, pitted and pocked — blithely
it bears the stretch-marks, scars and wrinkles
of longevity. Content to be used
by ice, wind and water, by men
who hollow it, quarry it, make it their own
habitation of cave or castle.

Impassively it sees them come and go,
the acorn germinate, the great oak fall.
It has mastered the art of stillness.

Beatrice Harrison Plays Her Cello to the Nightingale

Surrey. A garden, black and aromatic.
Woman and cello on the lawn
and somewhere an invisible bird.

We are all born for death, including
Beatrice and the nightingale.
Only the music aims at immortality:

the programmed throat endlessly reproduced,
the antique instrument, the record
updated with each new technology.

The cello hums its undersong
to the solo bird, whose voice is surprisingly loud —
a choirboy's effortless unvibrated treble.

With shut eyes she listens to herself
accompanying the legendary singer
that seems to fit its notes to hers

in a coincidence of languages. In truth,
like us, it speaks its own vocabulary of need
to its own kind.

Face

He and she in a room
with shadowy corners.
His gaze fixed on her face.
Her face lit like the moon.

He lays brightness on her
hair, forehead, cheekbone, chin
with lamp, spotlight, light-box,
luminous umbrella.

Mellows her radiance
with gold and silver screens
of creased cloth like mirrors
that hold no reflection.

For him, her face is skin
on a bone frame, surface
to be highlighted, glossed,
buffed up and presented.

And she must smile and smile
or all the lines point down.
He is hidden in gloom
behind a cyclops eye.

She imagines dark wall
opening like a door,
her lover looking out,
smiling. Her face kindles.

Catching Up

Two women
sixtyish, sitting
in a bright bay window,
talking, talking.

When I got near
I remembered the turn,
the wide street,
the well-proportioned house

which, thirty years ago
was full of children
and husbands.
Faces round the kitchen table.

The husbands have left,
the children grown and gone.
So much to say
and to leave unsaid.

The memories are bright
and circumscribed, like scenes
on television.
Was that happiness

or the quiet satisfactions
of now: the music, poetry,
travel, small indulgences,
careful plans?

The calm-faced women
have had enough of mothering.
Their lost men and children
must find their own directions.

Touch

The fingers travel down her spine impersonally intimate
checking off vertebrae. She thinks of dimples in dough.

Like a water-diviner the thumbs go straight
to the pain, probing the knot and the gritty crystals.

And now the heels of the hands are pressing and paring
the thick flesh down, remaking her, hollowing her waist.

They carry the sun's warmth and weight, the hot fume
of lavender fields, blue under blue. And there is birdsong,

music, silence. Then almost inaudibly the sounds again:
pan-pipes and temple bells and alpenhorn, echoey, breathy notes.

The fingers are gentling muscle, pushing, smoothing,
liquefying. Muscle on muscle, hands on flesh are sliding

fluent as fish, like lovers in their caul of sweat
skin to skin with no barriers or beginnings.

But now the fingertips are hard beads
at the base of her skull, then they are gone.

She sits up with a face drowse-burned and rosy,
her heaviness restored in rolls around her waist,

looseness of upper arms and puckered thighs,
and Mrs Bradby turning on the taps.

Postcards From the Gallery

One motif, two colours. Boys —
in each left hand a burning stick
that lights the face.

What cold fire the white boy blows
(watched by a monkey and a buck-toothed man).
His huge drooped eyelids are shadowy.

Red boy, almost in profile, pushes
his big lips out like a fish,
his face heavy and simple.

But I prefer the smudged ascetic one.
Pale boy's fire has a humdrum purpose.
Candle in the other hand — they need a light.

I don't trust the vermilion boy, with his bland absorption,
his little glinty eyes. The sort of boy who wouldn't
ask questions. Who'd sleep soundly
afterwards, whatever he'd been burning.

Little Fluffy Goes Native

He was a sweet suburban cat
who followed her around the flat
and slumbered on her bed at night
like a furry ammonite.

His coat, like a magician's cloak
in shades of caramel and smoke,
would ripple as he moved and shine,
its lines and circles intertwine.

If she went out he was bereft,
squeaked piteously when she left
and gazed at her with sad surprise
from his slanting yellow eyes.

He had a dainty appetite.
His gourmet meals must be just right:
chicken breast or tuna fish
chopped up in a special dish.

Then suddenly she moved. Henceforth
they were to live far in the north
in a cottage on a hill
where the wind blew strong and shrill.

At first the nervous cat lay curled
asleep all day. A savage world
might lie in wait for him outside
and monsters stalk the countryside.

One night he brought into the house
a tiny shrieking dark-eyed mouse,
one day a vole, the next day two.
One morning she found half a shrew

reclining on his supper plate.
Another morning laid out straight
in a row along the mat
four shrews, a mouse, a baby rat.

No longer would he deign to eat
her offerings. When she stroked his feet
she felt the ready claws. She saw
the needle teeth inside his jaw.

She quickly came to hate his habit
of bringing in a wounded rabbit.
Sometimes it crept away to hide,
tremble and bleed until it died.

Or if he killed it he would crunch
it up for breakfast or for lunch,
flesh, bones and fur; leave nothing but
four legs, a tail, a piece of gut.

He'd slink across the narrow track,
the dark stripes swaying on his back.
He took to staying out all day
and finally he stayed away.

She thinks of him out in the cold,
his eyes like bale-fires gleaming gold,
alert for falcon, dog or stoat,'
elusive in his shadow-coat.

Dissolution

I observed it working
the day I found the crippled rabbit
and lacked courage to kill it.
Saw the stoat slithering
away. Biding its time.
Later I heard the rabbit cry out
in a small human voice.

Next time the stoat kept still
as I came nearer.
Except for its rising choir of flies
it could have been sleeping
among the thyme and eyebright,
its body tubular, vivid ginger.
Neat flat ears and flywhisk tail.

Soon after, it had turned over,
sunk back on itself. A ribbon
of tan-edged cream. For weeks
I watched it shrink and fade
until all that marked it out
from the ground it lay on was
its miniature shark-mouth grin.

Sheep Show

No need to bring the camera — I have boxfuls
of interchangeable photographs of the same
strong-featured men, same Swaledale
sheep with washed black-and-white faces.

Some years there is this view of empty moor
stretching to Cumbria, other times only
a room hollowed from fog. At home there are pictures
of me here in a sheepskin coat, you in a Barbour,

me in short sleeves and sunhat, you raising a pint
of dark brown beer in the pub's dark interior.
Year on year the show goes on the same — tup classes
in ring number one, gimmers in two. Ewe, ram,

shearling and hogg go down immortal
through time, shown by the same names —
Metcalfe and Calvert, Harker and Alderson —
played in by the same brass band

to the same field full of landrovers, fences,
rocky outcrops, trimmed hummocks and dung,
that I know so well I shan't need to come next year
when you have gone away to the far side of the globe.

The Fruit-Eaters

His neat teeth bite into a giant plum
piercing thin skin, slicing off golden flesh.
She watches from the other side of the room.
In her own mouth she senses the gush
of sweetness that delights his agile tongue
and the aftershock of tartness that will wring
the cheek's lining. She nibbles her pear. It is bland,
pearly inside. She sees that the close-grained
skin of his muscular forearm and the hand that cups
and offers up the plum are warmly brown,
but his inner arm is virginal white.
She thinks of tanned fingers on a breast. His lips
open, then meet together, stretch for the fruit
and close, until all that is left is a stone.

Oh Speak Again, Bright Angel!

Like the voice of the sea in a shell
his voice in the telephone, tiny and intimate.
Which is shell, which is ear?

Every time, she presses 2 to save it.
*Your message will be saved for thirty —
twenty-four — twenty-one —fifteen days.*

Is repetition wearing it away?
His voice is flat, devoid of his energy
and shine. But it is his, his northern vowels

his slight lisps and blurrings. A banal
message, formulaic, but all she has.
She presses 1 to hear it again. *First saved*

*message. Message received Thursday,
April, 10th, at, 4.53, pm.*
Waiting, she holds her breath.

Lover

Whiteness at the curtain's edge. After midnight
and she can't sleep. Pulls back the heavy cloth.

Full moon is piercingly bright
above the indigo rim

of hills. She brings his picture to the light
looking for comfort in the long soft mouth,

fine curve of jaw. But a blight
of moonshine has withered him.

The gaunt white face might
be bone. Eyes swallowed in sockets of blackness.

The Love-Token

Tight as asparagus or exotic grain
the budded stems parcelled in darkness.
A long way from the hedged fields
of home, the sieved sea-wind.

Oh, these have a raging thirst
after their journey. White or yellow
petals thin as skin unfold,
turn to six-pointed stars so small

you can't imagine them dancing.
Even in their native breeze
they would only shiver. Breath
of spring, fugitive scent of honey,

vanilla, sap, in a minor key.
But the centrally heated stillness
will crisp them. Tomorrow's sun
will light a host of little dead faces.

Washing the Teaset

Anxious ghost, my grandmother stands beside me
eyeing the china. I am washing her wedding teaset,
mine now, dulled with years of dust and breath.

Each piece sings a different musical note.
Gold-ringed translucent white, patterned with stylised
vegetation in muted blue, green, brown.

There are two big plates, shaped like shallow bowls
for sacramental bread and butter. Basin and jug.
Twelve side-plates, saucers. And eleven cups.

Was there a terrible hush, the small suppressed boy
sent to his room (supper smuggled up later by mother)?
Or a slip in the scullery suds, a day of heartache?

I wonder if Emmy chose these impractical things
as a message to Arthur's superior sisters? Or did he
in his huge surgical boot hanker after their lightness?

She kept them for best. Cherished this porcelain
as she cherished the precious and only child.
It will be safe, I assure her, as your son was.

His wife, his daughters, the kind Lancashire nurses
tended him gently, safeguarding his end
as you did his beginning. Rest, his life is completed.

And look — I have arranged these brittle relics,
that he kept for fifty years to remember you,
out of harm's way behind glass, where nothing can touch them.

Travelling

In the Black Forest the brownshirts saluted them: Heil Hitler!
— hard to keep a straight face. Then his wartime wanderings:
North Africa, Sicily, dot-to-dot up the map of Italy
with a smattering of the language.

For her it was nineteen years of the Home Front. Chancy weather
in Wales or Cornwall. But he remembered the melting heat, wine,
lemons on trees, and after the lean years they were off
in the Mayflower, the Vanguard, the Sunbeam

pushing further south each year or taking to the air like birds
towards the wine-dark waters: Adriatic, Ionian, Nile.
But now the holiday slides in their labelled boxes
fade undisturbed under the eaves,

projector and its paraphernalia too cumbersome to carry.
Today he walked as far as the church bench, leaning his small weight
on his mother's stick, but couldn't get up again and across the cobbles
without the strong hand of a stranger.

Christmas Presents

She gave him a fleece waistcoat, dove-grey and feather-soft.
He could never get warm. If you held his bruised arthritic hand
it was an icy claw.

He gave her — and she chose it — a bracelet
of polished gold rhomboids and cut amethysts
with hook and ring fastening.

In the box it glows on the black velvet. You could imagine
stone and metal softening under the light. But to do up
hook and golden eye

with one hand and poor vision is too hard,
his bent fingers too clumsy. And when
did she think she'd ever wear it?

The zip on the waistcoat must be faulty.
Somehow he has done it up crooked. She shouts at him
that he has broken it, so they can't take it back.

Sunday Afternoon

Larchlap fencing with trellis on top
too high to look over and shaky in a wind
because the old man hasn't noticed the broken post.

Summer has outlived itself and the September gardens
seem steeped in honey: the warm colour
of the leaning fence, the little wooden bench

he is sitting on, the drowsy afternoon.
On the other side of the fence Graham, Jackie and Jessica
are bringing out a late lunch, calling, clattering cutlery.

Here in his corner my father is still, slumped.
The gentle sunlight warms his shut eyelids, the fallen
flesh of his face. He is breathing so quietly we are not sure:

two daughters equally still, watching with identical tension,
deciding in whispers not to call the ambulance
yet again, in the unspoken hope dying might be this easy.

Hospital Visit

That white hill, glistening, insistent, looms over
the little town. I had never noticed
it was so close — stripped of its cloudy greys.

He lies on the hospital bed, thankful
to be there at last, his face a very pale
yellow as if lit by the winter sun

that sheens the slope of snow outside, smoothly
as Christmas icing. I know I can go
now, leaving him in good hands. At the road junction

I look right, into an avenue of brilliance
in which I can see nothing at all.
To my dazzled eyes the heart of light is darkness.

Thistledown

They have criss-crossed my window for weeks now,
colourless on dull days, silver in the sun,
small hazy globes like thoughts.

Catch one in your hands — so light,
so unlike a captive butterfly, it is
more spirit than substance.

Today, as I climb the hill against the wind
carrying his ashes, thistledown flies past me
shining and purposeful.

Some of it travels miles, some falls in drifts
of ghost-snow round the ruined spires. I turn
and shake his ashes out towards the sun.

Cuthbert and the Sea-Otters

Night is freedom. His feet
make light of the chilly sand
and the salt shallows.

His neck in the noose of the North Sea:
after the pain, an absence of body,
the head floats in emptiness.

Sometimes the moon frosts his skull
or stars hang over him
like never-arriving hailstones,

but black still nights are best.
He drifts back through the days of creation
to darkness on the face of the deep

and the spirit stroking the water.
Just before dawn his eyes see in the dark
and he can hear in the complete silence.

It is returning that hurts:
his shoulders rise into the whip of wind
as the world fills him again.

He streams with brine as if weeping all over.
Sea-otters try to comfort him
with their small breath and body warmth.

Setting Out

1. Stranded

The pilgrims pace up and down the East Quay
or the West Quay. When the tide goes out, the river
is green-brown mud with a sheen and smell.
Twice a day the river fills, empties,
but still the small boats slump in their places.

This journey is meaningless without arrival.
Unsure if God exists, the travellers
await the revelations of completion.
Listlessly they climb high on the down
to the ruined chapel and gaze out over the shoreline

to where the sister chapel has vanished
long since from the rough summit —
threatened now by bramble and sycamore —
of the almost-hemispherical island
riding at anchor on the chancy sea.

They long to set out into themselves,
to advance into the past, to re-live
as in a dream, over and over, love, death,
disillusionment, childhood. They need to recover
the innocence of rockpools, springwater, spray-filtered air.

Over there, seagulls dance at dawn on the tarred roofs
of the huts, their voices variously human: cursing,
pleading, grieving, as if recollected emotion
could turn into music. At the end of the day they achieve
stillness, poised on the empty beach staring into the wind.

2. Next Year. Embarking

a.

A hot drive down, but on arrival
at the East Quay, harbouring its fishing fleet,
the view dissolves. Uppermost
of the heaped houses soften
to semi-visible. Shock
of the known world thinning,
and out to sea our destination cancelled.

Faith is setting off in an open boat
into emptiness (the boatman
promising nothing.) The mainland pales,
falls silent, fades out altogether
like a reverse polaroid.
All around, whiteness,
the rocking gleam of water.

The boat turns abruptly. Are we going back?
Is nothing all there is?
But from the wrong direction
a greyer hump of cloud, a ghost-island
expands and darkens. And there,
dreamlike, the small familiar beach
below the brooding wood.

Rasp of the prow's grounding
jars us back to reality.
Jumping on to the shingle,
heaving gangplank, hefting baggage. Too busy
to drop down on our knees
and kiss the cold, damp,
seaweed-smelling landfall.

Embarking

b.

In the small dark hours
I am woken by
a constant humming
like a long-drawn-out
cello-note,

the ramshackle room
full of it. Is it
inside my head?
I step out on to
wet black grass.

Air is sharply clear
and lights are gliding
on glassy water,
white lights and green lights
steadily

processing, strung out
evenly on their
bass continuo,
towards an unseen
horizon.

Endings

The old queen has not seen the back of her island
for years. Its shining grasses
grow feathery, five-foot, golden, break and lie.
Brambles burst out in jewelled fruit
that falls and rots. Gulls in their thousands
breed and die, breed and die on the spattered cliffs.

She can glimpse the south shore across an abandoned room,
gaze from the doorway towards the line
where blue and blue meet, or where the lower grey
and upper dissolve together, and wish
the island could slip its moorings, be her burial-
ship out to that far or lost horizon.

She can watch the birds floating on thermals. There
a herring gull banks slightly, levels itself
with a tremor that runs along its underside,
then glides into the sun, its tail
and ailerons translucent, head alight.

There was once a chapel here, but long ago
the island swallowed it. The hill is empty.
Only a couple of unwieldy stones left lying.

Children have grown here, shed their childhoods, gone.
Love has been found; bathed in like phosphorescence
in midnight water; lost. And all the past is a blur
of superimposed transparencies.
The island is heartless, shrugs off love and joy
and grief indifferently, like seasons.

The house, too, has turned on her, its rooms silted
and stuffed with hoarded trash. The queen
for a moment dreams revenge. The summer grasses,
the old trees tinder dry. All could go up
with her in a splendid pyre. But it doesn't matter.
She looks at her old, old hands. The sky darkens
and moon springs up like a bloody thumbprint.
A short wait, and it will all be over.

SHAKESPEARE'S LOST LADIES

1. Queen Lear

Does it corrupt? Perhaps. But certainly
power kills common sense. I say nothing.
I save my breath. Of course, he wanted boys,
viewed Goneril and Regan merely as
marriage-fodder. And when Cordelia
(his little princess) came along, he was
in his dotage, never even noticed
the tight-lipped elder sisters. No good
will come of these resentments, I thought. What
blaze could give my daughters satisfaction?
Fading before their eyes, insubstantial
as cloud, I can provide nothing they want.
And he, always weak-brained, is stupefied
by the fat perfume of sacrifices.
Not for him the harsh battle or sluggish
council-chamber. He delights in feasting
in the hall with candle-flames numerous
as stars, and the tame poet singing songs
of his imaginary heroics.

2. Donalbain's Mother

I killed her. First act of my life. And now my father's dead.
(Shall I be accused of that?) And just now, when my brother
and I had our hasty conference (I'll to England. To Ireland I)
I thought , madly, why not add fratricide, then I'll be king?

Dear mother! what is happening? Something in this place
is painting my thoughts scarlet. She never spoke to me,
they said. Never moved after my birth. I think of her
lying bright white in a bed of blood.

I only know her through others. "Oftener upon her knees
than on her feet/died every day she lived",
is the tag everyone couples with her name. Why
was she more nun than queen? What had she done

that needed such endless cleansing? And was she happy
to die for real? I think of her as made of light, like angels,
her oval face a candle flame. Guide me then, mother,
out of this dark predicament.

3. Signora Brabantio

Not the name I am known by now, but no need
to cause embarrassment. So she's broken out,
has she? Done a runner, as I did, from Venice
where the huddled palazzi seem to be jostling
for position; obsessed with appearances.
It was hard to breathe in his house, the sluggish air
tainted always with a whiff of canal.

I was sorry to leave her, my pale, placid daughter,
good little convent-schoolgirl. But she would be safe
there as a jewel in a case, a sleeper
in a goosedown bed. The general's stories
would have threaded her days like pleasant dreams.
There's something enchanting about a swarthy man
for the true North Italian phlegmatic blonde.

But a soldier? How will she cope without
her padded luxury? An African?
How will she read the dark glass of his mind?

4. Lady Polonius

I don't go out. Why should I want to?
Elsinore is a place of whispers:
mutterings in the chimney,
voices behind tapestries. Listen,
on a still night the battlements are talking.

You thought I was dead. Sometimes
I think so too, if ghosts can walk
and suffer. They tell me I am sick,
not dead. Still, I shall not go out.
They are discussing me behind their hands.

So many words, but I can't find out
what is happening. This is because
the words are lies, or in a foreign language.
For all I know my husband may be dead
though he jabbers at me all night in my dreams.

My son has gone. O stay away, stay away —
in Elsinore the air is poisoned.
My daughter is out of her wits with calf-love.
I open my mouth to warn her
but all that comes out is the chirping of birds.

5. Duchess of Milan

The best day of my life — and the last
if I am held to my promise.
Now as the day darkens we are left
alone. Your father, that stranger
who only lives inside his mind,
has visited and gone.
Your eyes are opening. Look,
Miranda, miracle child,
this is your mother's face
which you will not remember.

Often in dreams I have seen my babies
laid out in a row, all white,
all still, and as I touch each face
the yielding skin hardens to marble.
This birth was different. The small life
inside me insisted on itself,
fought for the air. I made a bargain
with fate. If we two owe a death
let it be mine. And you were born alive,
breathing and warm.

I have given you what I can
and now you are cast out
on a world of danger to grow up
like a flower in a desert place
marked "Here be monsters" on some
unreliable map.

6. Princess Escalus

Some shall be pardon'd and some punished.
Discuss. But nobody chooses Escalus
as a candidate for punishment. Why not?
I ask myself. Is he above the law?
No, no, you say. He did his best. Did he?
He did what he always does — which is to wait
till everyone's there, the drama at its height,
and make an entrance, on a white charger
preferably. The pullulating hordes
fall silent, mouths open in awe, abashed.
Then from his lofty seat he reprimands
and threatens: "Do this again and I'll... I'll..."
But it was no use giving little pep-talks
to old Lord Montague, doddering Capulet.
Their ancient feud had taken on a life
of its own, unstoppable, its origins
forgotten, not the point any longer. I
could see that. Why couldn't he, then? Tybalt was
a psychopath who could not be controlled
by his elders or himself. Young Romeo,
testosterone's slave, chasing a different girl
every day of the week, was, I suppose,
egged on by dainty skirted Lawrence who
would stroke his cheeks to wipe away the tears
and promise to sort all his problems out.
My husband's relatives drop like flies — Paris,
Mercutio — and what does he do? More threats?
A banishment? Oh please! Verona is
tiny. A murderer outside the walls
is still a menace. But the prince retires
calmly to bed and seems surprised, aggrieved,
to be woken early by more tragedy.
He stands pontificating in the street
apportioning blame with undisturbed conceit.

7. Lost Ladies

We are the faceless ladies
wearing masks
age cannot wither.
The wind blew
and our emotions froze
into bland sadness.
Our eyewhites are china
with a hole at the centre.
Is there anything
looking out?
We could have been
catalysts in the action,
or commented on it
like a Greek chorus,
but our mouths
are empty ellipses.

We are bargaining counters,
breeding machines,
trophy wives,
to be stashed away
in attics, salons,
mausoleums,
curtained beds.
Seed is put into
and children come out
of our vaporous bodies,
hidden now
under floor-length gowns
like shameful secrets.
Even our names
are leaving us
anonymous.

HELOISE DREAMING

1.

magistro suo nobilissimo atque doctissimo *

The study: a shelf of sleeping books,
stringed instrument silently observing
the man in black, his taut distinguished face,
the girl crying deliciously on his shoulder.
So young the pink eyelids and nose-tip
are endearing not ugly. Below her rosy mouth
a redness like a little flower, chin-burn
from too much kissing of a long-jawed man.
In front of her on the desk the open volume
pushed crooked, disregarded. Logic,
which orders this chaotic world, unprized
by the stung lips, greedily reaching hands.
The universals have slunk into their kennels
while eyes, tongues, nostrils search out
and taste the tiniest particulars.

And yet you always had that desert fathers'
austerity in you, pulling you away,
kindling self-disgust, tainting your mouth, afterwards,
with the word *lust*. And when nemesis struck,
I imagine your first sound, on waking,
neither scream nor howl but a sigh —
of relief? thankfulness? An absolution
you had not looked for, a way back
into the passion of reasoning. But I,
living a penance for a life, could not repent.
I burned, and was glad.

* to her most noble and learned teacher

2.

iocunde spei mee *

Now you are here to stay I think of you
transubstantiated to pure whiteness
of bone: the long bones of the leg;
the delicate finger-bones; the curved
ribs once cradling lungs that made breath
for the caress and charm of language.

I kneel beside your grave. Do you remember
that first night when you held my hand
under the table, interlaced my fingers
with yours until our bones burned?
I kept my face pious and bland as you talked on,
weaving your spell over the old men.

Now through the thinning skin I see
the nineteen bones of my hand ready themselves
for when unnecessary flesh
shall vanish like spring snow
and my clean bones and yours will fall
together and be undistinguishable.

* *to my joyful hope*

3.

thesauro suo incomparabili *

You say it was lust, but it was your mind
that walked towards me, your bright intelligence
in your eyes, your kisses, the words
of your lips, your desperation.
Impossible to divide spirit and flesh. My soul
with its lips and limbs revelled in yours.
I loved you with my skin, blood and interior organs
and when your touch was lost to me for ever
I couldn't hold your essence in my spirit-hands,
you ran from me like water. Now my thoughts
are all of the many textures of skin,
your sweat that made us slippery as fishes,
your weight, heat, your mouth tasting of apples.
In the candle-light your body: dark gold
as a precious artefact. You smiled at me
with a child's unclouded smile.
In each of your eyes a tiny flame.

* *to her incomparable treasure*

4.

lumini clarissimo et solsticio suo *

I dreamed of you exiled beside the sea.
From a high window the cliff-bound bay
is a bowl of stars.

Your back against the brilliance,
you lean into the room.
I can see the illuminated rim
of forehead, cheek and jaw, the sharp
peak of one knee under black fabric,
one bony hand intensely arguing.

I strain to see your lips, your eyes in shadow.
I strain to hear your magical words
but there is only silence.

Waking, I remember waking and watching you
bathed in another window's milder light,
standing relaxed, naked,
a fair-skinned man, shaving
by a basin, with a golden fuzz
all round your body, as if you were shining.

* *to her brightest light and solstice*

5.

hucusque dilecto semperque diligendo *

I dreamed I was dead. My ghost ran crying for you
through a house with many rooms and corridors.
I found you beside your shelf of books in a study
lit by a hundred candles, knelt beside you
and said *I love you*. You said *God forbid*,
turning to me with eyes as clear as water.

It was an arranged marriage. I the reluctant bride
of Christ, propelled to the altar.
Such marriages can be successful
so I grieved and waited, but without intention
what hope? I have already had
a lifetime's blessings. Spiritual aspirations
are a fantasy landscape scarcely there:
cumulus trees, hills covered in ghost snow.

I shroud my ageing body in coarse black,
too cold, too hot, a torment to the skin.
I have no life but a labour. I rise first
for the midnight office and for lauds at sunrise,
encourage my sisters in the draughty chapel:
grey faces, shivering draperies. Sleeplessness
and fasting may blunt the pangs of memory, lull
the already mortified flesh.

* *to one loved until now and always to be loved*

6.

amori suo precordiali *

Dead. But your posthumous words
insist on living. I can see them, touch them,
brownish-black on the parchment.

It's not so much that I hear your voice,
that almost-overlaid regional accent —
it's the you-ness of thought and image

tightens my skin and windpipe.
I know what will come next and see
the shapes your ghost-mouth makes

as if you spoke to me alone,
you and I islanded on a bed
in a bubble of candle-light.

Outside, the perilous cold
and darkness, footsteps, cries
of the insomniac city.

* *to her heart's love*

7.

vale spiraculum meum *

This morning I woke from a dream I could not remember.
Outside my window the short grass, transfixed
by heavy dew, white with a slight shimmer,
stretched unprinted like the beginning of love.
I knew that under my bare feet it would be
an effervescence of icy light.

If you first saw me now, you would not love me.
Would not be charmed by the little cushions
above and below my waist, my face stiffened,
set, as if most of the possibilities had departed.

In fact, I was never beautiful, though you called me
beautiful. I was only a round-faced girl.
All I had was youth, an untouched freshness
yours to imprint and use for your pleasure.

And yet I loved your greying temples,
your thinning crown, the coarse pores of your nose.
Loved not so much your famed beauty
as your advertised mortality.

I watched you sleeping one afternoon, the quick cursive
and tension of your expressive face erased away,
the furies that drove you taking a break.
On the sundial the finger of shadow paused.
All I wanted was to watch over you,
synchronise my breathing with your quiet breath.

* *goodbye, my breath*